D0803445

LMH Official Dictionary of

JAMAICAN
HISTORY

Compiled by

L. Mike Henry / K. Sean Harris

LMH PUBLISHING LIMITED

© 2004 LMH Publishing Limited
First Edition
10 9 8 7 6 5 4 3 2 1
2006 Revised
2009 Reprint
10 9 8 7 6 5 4 3
2013 Revised Edition
10 9 8 7 6 5 4
2016 Revised Edition
10 9 8 7 6 5

Compiled by: K. Sean Harris / L. Mike Henry
Cover Design: Lee-Quee Design and Sanya Dockery
Design & Typesetting: PAGE Services and Sanya Dockery

Published by: LMH Publishing Limited
Suite 10-11, Sagicor Industiral Park
7 Norman Road
Kingston C.S.O., Jamaica
Tel: 876-938-0005   Fax: 876-759-8752
Email: lmhbookpublishing@cwjamaica.com
Webside: www.lmhpublishing.com

Printed in China   ISBN: 978-976-8202-97-0

CONTENTS

INTRODUCTION

Jamaica is the largest English speaking island in the Caribbean. It is 150 miles long and approximately 50 miles at its widest point, covering an area of 4,411 square miles. The interior is mountainous and gives rise to many rivers. The Blue Mountains, running east to west, reach a peak of 7, 402 ft.

The island has a maritime tropical climate and temperatures range from approximately 80 degrees – 90 degrees at sea level and from 50 to 60 degrees in the mountains. June through September are the warmest months and the traditionally rainy months are May and October.

Jamaica's original inhabitants are the Taino Indians who came from South America some 2500 years ago. They named the island 'Xaymaca', which meant 'land of wood and water'. Christopher Columbus came upon the island in 1494 and claimed it for Spain. The Spaniards substituted the X for J and the island became Jamaica. The Tainos were a gentle, peaceful people who loved dancing, hunting and playing ball games. The Taino population was totally wiped out by the brutality of the Spanish settlers. They were replaced with African slaves.

The island was invaded in 1655 by a British expedition who had failed to conquer Santo Domingo. Instead of going away empty handed, they took Jamaica as a consolation prize. The African slaves of the Spanish colonists escaped into the hills and lived a free life. They were called the Maroons. They harassed the British conquerors to such an extent that they were granted independence and their own lands by treaty in 1734, and are in part autonomous even today.

English is the official and commercial language, although a local Patois is widely spoken. The vast majority of Jamaicans are of African descent of a mixed race of Negroes, Indians, Caucasians and Chinese. Jamaica has more churches per square mile than anywhere else in the world. The largest religious body is Anglican. Others include Baptists, Roman Catholics, Methodists, Presbyterians, Judaism, Buddhism, Revivalism, Seventh Day Adventists and Moravians. There are also other religious groups such as Hindus, Muslims, Bahai's and Rastafarians.

Jamaica has two major political parties, the People's National Party formed in 1938; and the Jamaica Labour Party formed in 1943. The road to self government was paved in 1944, when adult suffrage was granted to all people of the age of 21 and over, giving them the right to vote. The first election under Universal Adult Suffrage was held in 1944 and the Jamaica Labour Party was victorious in the polls.

In January 1962, a draft of the Independence Constitution was unanimously approved. At midnight, August 5, 1962, the British flag was lowered and the Jamaican flag was hoisted for the first time. On August 6, 1962, Jamaica became an independent nation.

EMBLEMS OF
NATIONHOOD

The National Flag of Jamaica

The colours are black, green and gold. A symbol of unity, the Black represents strength and creativity; the Green represents hope and agricultural resources, and the Gold symbolizes natural wealth and the beauty of sunshine.

The National Pledge

Before God and all mankind, I
pledge the love and loyalty of
my heart, the wisdom and
courage of my mind, the
strength and vigour of my
body in the service of my
fellow citizens. I promise to
standup for Justice,
Brotherhood and Peace, to
work diligently and
creatively, to think generously
and honestly, so that Jamaica
may, under God, increase in
beauty, fellowship and
prosperity, and play her part
in advancing the welfare of
the whole human race.

The National Coat of Arms

The original coat of arms was designed by William Sandcroft, a former Canterbury Archbishop. The orginal Latin motto, Indus Uterque Serveit Uni, was changed and Jamaicanized to Out of Many One People.

The National Anthem

Eternal Father, bless our land,
Guard us with Thy Mighty Hand,
Keep us free from evil powers,
Be our light through countless hours.
To our leaders, Great Defender,
Grant true wisdom from above.
Justice, truth be ours forever,
Jamaica, land we love.
Jamaica, Jamaica, Jamaica,
land we love.

Teach us true respect for all,
Stir response to duty's call,
Strengthen us the weak to cherish,
Give us vision lest we perish.
Knowledge send us Heavenly Father,
Grant true wisdom from above.
Justice, truth be ours forever,
Jamaica, land we love.
Jamaica, Jamaica, Jamaica,
land we love.

The Streamer Tailed Humming Bird

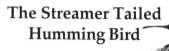

(Doctor Bird)
Trochilus polytmus
(Second smallest bird in the world)

Ackee Fruit

Blighia sapida
(The main
ingredient of
Jamaica's
national dish,
Ackee and Saltfish)

Blue Mahoe
Hibiscus elatus

Lignum Vitae Flower
Guaiacum officinale

JAMAICA'S
PRIME MINISTERS

The Rt. Excellent Norman Washington Manley, Q.C., LI.B., and National Hero served as Jamaica's Chief Minister and Premier immediately prior to independence. He died in 1969 at the age of 76.

The Rt. Excellent Sir William Alexander Bustamante, Kt. P.C., G.B.E., LI.D., and National Hero was Jamaica's first Prime Minister. He served for one and a half terms and retired from Parliament at the age of 80. He died in 1977 at the age of 93 and was buried with national and international honours.

The Most Honourable Sir Donald Burns Sangster, O.N., K.C.V.O., LI.B., finished Bustamante's second term but died after being Prime Minister for only a month.

The Most Honourable Hugh Lawson Shearer, O.N., P.C., M.P., was Jamaica's third Prime Minister. He was the BITU's island supervisor when Sangster died and he assumed the role of Prime Minister by a decision against his colleagues Clem Tavares and Robert Lightbourne.

The Most Honourable Michael Norman Manley, O.N., P.C., B.Sc., became Prime Minister in 1972. His first two terms in office were characterized by social programs and alliances with socialist governments. Illness forced him to retire from politics in 1992 and he died in 1997.

The Most Honourable Edward Phillip George Seaga, O.N., P.C., M.P., B.A, was Jamaica's fourth Prime Minister. He served in office from 1980-1989 and he was Jamaica's longest serving Member of Parliament, having won his Western Kingston seat in 1962 and retained it until his retirement in 2005.

The Most Honourable Percival James (P.J.) Patterson, O.N., P.C., Q.C., M.P., B.A., LL.B., became Prime Minister when Manley retired in 1992. He led the People's National Party to an unprecedented fourth term in office.

The Most Honourable Orette Bruce Golding, M.P., became Jamaica's eighth Prime Minister following the Jamaica Labour Party's (JLP) slim victory in the 2007 general election held on September 3rd. He served for four years before resigning on October 2011, becoming the first Prime Minister in the history of Jamaica to do so.

The Most Honourable Andrew Michael Holness, O.N., M.P., is the youngest person to become Prime Minister (age 39) in Jamaica's history. He was Jamaica's ninth Prime Minister and also Jamaica's second shortest serving Prime Minister, having served from October 2011 to December 2011.

The Most Honourable Portia Lucretia Simpson Miller,
O.N., M.P., B.A., became Jamaica's first female Prime
Minister when Patterson retired in March, 2006. She
also created history by becoming the first female President-
elect of the People's National Party (PNP) in February
of the same year. On December 29, 2011, she was
elected as Prime Minister of Jamaica for a second time,
when her party defeated the Andrew Holness led Jamaica
Labour Party in the general election. She assumed office
on January 5, 2012.

The Most Honourable Andrew Michael Holness, O.N.,
M.P., became Prime Minister for the second time
on March 3, 2016 following the February 25, 2016
general elections when he led the Jamaica Labour
Party to a historical victory by a one-seat majority.
He is the first Prime Minister to be born post-
Jamaica's independence. His wife, Juliet Holness,
became a Member of Parliament, making it the
first time a Prime Minister and wife duo served in
Parliament.

JAMAICA'S GOVERNORS-GENERAL

The role of the Governor-General is primarily a ceremonial one. Among his ceremonial duties are the oath of office to parliamentarians, judges and public servants of senior rank and appointing to life-long service the Custodes for the fourteen parishes.

These Custodes perform ceremonial roles on behalf of the Governor-General and are the responsible body for the confirmation of the appointments of Justices of the Peace.

Sir Kenneth Blackburn (1957-1962): Jamaica's last English Governor who saw the transfer of colonial rule to independence and who served as Governor-General in the last months before independence from July 1962.

Sir Clifford Campbell (1962-1973): Jamaica's first native Governor-General.

Sir Florizel Glasspole (1973-1991): Late former Jamaican Governor-General who retired from the post in 1991.

His Excellency, The Most Honourable Sir Howard Cooke (1991-2006): Became Jamaica's third native Governor-General on August 1, 1991.

His Excellency, The Most Honourable Sir Kenneth Hall, (2006-2009): Became Governor-General in February 2006.

His Excellency, The Most Honourable Sir Patrick Allen, (2009 – present): Jamaica's sixth Governor-General and the fifth Jamaican to hold this position since independence (1962).

A

Abolition: In July of 1833, some 450,000 enslaved blacks in the West Indies were made free men with the effective date of the Emancipation Act being August 1st, 1834. Slavery was not fully abolished in Jamaica until 1838 due to the slaves having to serve for another four years under an apprenticeship programme.

Absenteeism: The term which describes the custom of planters and owners of estates residing overseas.

Ackee: This fruit is consumed with salt fish as the national dish of Jamaica and is also the national fruit. The fruit must be allowed to ripen on the tree, otherwise it could be poisonous. This versatile fruit has several medicinal and other uses, a few of which are: The leaves can be used to make a tea for colds, flu and mucus congestion. The skin of the ackee can be beaten to a pulp and used as a kind of soap.

African Slavery: The system practised in West Africa, and was essentially a benevolent slavery as against chattel slavery of the West Indies.

Alternative Crops: The food crops grown by the freed slaves after Emancipation, i.e. coffee, ginger, nutmeg and coconuts.

Amerindians: The original settlers of the American continents. The Arawaks and the Caribs were the tribes that settled in the Caribbean.

Anancy: Also spelled Anansi, is the Jamaican name for spider. The name comes directly from the West African name *Ananse*. Anancy is the main character of the folk tales referred to as Anancy stories. In these folk tales, Anansi is depicted as a spider with human-like qualities and characteristics. He is a greedy yet loveable trickster who triumphs over his enemies by using his cunning and wit. Anancy stories are a part of the Jamaican oral tradition and have endured for thousands of years. Traditional storytelling has decreased in popularity in recent times, however, there are many books that preserve the Anansi stories. (Read 'Anancy Mek It' -Peter Paul Zahl; 'Confessions of Anansi'-David Brailsford; 'Anancy & Friends'-Beulah Richmond).

Anglican Church: The official church of the British West Indies and the planter class.

Apprenticeship: Period of transition between the abolition of slavery and Emancipation.

EXTERIOR OF ST. PETER ANGLICAN CHURCH

ARAWAK GIRL
(COURTESY OF THE NATIONAL LIBRARY OF JAMAICA)

Aqueduct: Cut stone waterway which carried water to the sugar mills from the source.

Arawaks: (Tainos) Gentle Amerindians whom the Spanish decimated, and who have given us such items as the hammock, and bammy.

Areito: A communal music and dance ceremony of the Arawaks. This ceremony was performed to mark important events of their lives. Areitos varied in size, but usually involved hundreds of participants who would dance in concentric circles around a group of musicians playing instruments such as the *mayohabo*, a large slit drum.

Auction: Method used to sell African slaves.

B

Babylon: The Rastafarian symbol for the oppressors of the poor and disenfranchised, as well as the place of oppression.

Backra: Term used to describe a white planter.

Bagasse: The dried cane trash, crushed from the mill, and used to fuel the boiling house, where the juice of the sugarcane was turned into molasses.

Baibrama: This Arawak God (Zemis) was the spirit of vegetation and fertility. His name meant 'Lord of the Harvest'. Baibrama was usually represented with a small bowl on his head that was used to hold offerings.

Bammy: Flat cake made from the cassava plant. Bammy is a staple Jamaican food and is generally eaten with fried fish.

Banana: The fruit grown after Emancipation, and which transformed the Jamaican society by the growth of the ports at Manchioneal, Oracabessa, Port Morant, and Port Antonio, and gave rise to the Jamaican Railway, which was the first Railway built outside of Great Britain, and built within 10 years of James Watts invention of the Steam Engine. By 1930 Jamaica was earning some $2 million annually from the export of bananas, which was approximately 57% of Jamaica's export.

Baptists: An early non-conformist denomination that was an active anti-slavery group, who were very instrumental in establishing free villages in Jamaica. Known missionaries were, William Knibb, Thomas Burchell, John Smith and lay preacher, Sam Sharpe.

Batos: A game played by the Arawaks, which required the players on both sides to try to put a rubber ball through a stone ring.

Bauxite: Discovered in the 1860s. In the 1950s Jamaica became the leading exporter of this product, controlling some 20% of the world's export.

THE RT. EXCELLENT SIR WILLIAM ALEXANDER BUSTAMANTE,
KT. P.C., G.B.E., LI.D.

Bogle, Paul: (1825-1865) National Hero of Jamaica. He led the Morant Bay Rebellion in 1865. He led the march from Stony Gut to Morant Bay protesting the poor living conditions of Jamaicans. This resulted in the burning of the Court House and the death of 20 people. He was hanged on 23rd October, 1865. He was made a National Hero in 1969.

Boiling House: The most important part of the sugar factory, where the actual boiling of the cane juice took place.

Breadfruit: Unknown in Jamaica before 1793, the breadfruit tree is widely grown and has a wide range of uses. The fruit is edible and may be prepared in a number of ways. The leaves and the sap which runs from the tree can be used for various ailments.

Bucaneers: Mainly British and French citizens who operated from Port Royal and Tortuga. This led to Port Royal being called the wickedest city on Earth. Leading proponents were Mary Price, Anne Bonney, Blackbeard and Henry Morgan, who in the 1670s became Lt. Governor of Jamaica.

Bustamante, Sir Alexander: (1884-1977) First Prime Minister of Jamaica and National Hero. Born Alexander Clarke in Blenheim, Hanover, he founded the BITU and the Jamaica Labour Party in 1943 and was incarcerated for leading the fight against low wages. He is the only one of seven (7) National Heroes to have been named National Hero while still alive.

SPANISH TOWN SQUARE

C

Cacique: The leader of the Arawaks who kept the society together and led in a multi-faceted role.

Cane Piece: The area on the estate used to plant sugar cane.

Caribs: The warlike tribe who constantly at-tacked the Arawaks, stealing their women and their food, and who still survive in St. Vincent and Dominica.

Cassava: Also known as manioc. It is used to make bammy.

Chinese: They migrated to the West Indies between 1838-82 as indentured labourers, from such areas as Macao and Taipeng.

Christmas Rebellion: On 27th December 1831, enslaved blacks in St. James rebelled

11

against slavery – led by Sam Sharpe. They decided to stop working and remain on strike until they were guaranteed freedom. By 1832 bands of slaves roamed Cornwall County and the uprising spread to Trelawny. With the battles raging the British called on the Maroons, who were bound by Treaty, to assist in returning the rebels, and this combined with an amnesty, undermined the rebellion. By 5th, February 1832 over 1000 enslaved blacks had been killed and 14 whites. Some 312 blacks were executed after the Montego Bay Square Sham trials found them guilty. The leader, Sam Sharpe, was himself hanged. The square is named after him.

Colonial Architecture: The style of architecture introduced to the West Indies during slavery. The colonial style of Western Europe such as Georgian, were adapted in keeping with the tropical climate. Evidence of this is seen in the Great Houses built by planters. The Spanish Town Square and Falmouth in Trelawny are inspiring examples of this form of architecture, with cut stone, seasoned mahogany and logwood being the chief materials.

Colony: Countries which were possessions of the English, French, Dutch and Spanish, between 1492 and the twentieth Century, of which Jamaica was one until 1964.

Columbus (1451-1506): Born in Genoa, Italy. He made four voyages to the West Indies claiming lands for his Queen and spreading the growth of Catholicism.

Conuco: Arawak name for the agricultural plots in which seeds and cuttings were planted in mounds.

Coyaba: The Arawak heaven – The Arawaks believed that their spirits went to this wonderful place.

Cricket: A game imported from England to the British Colonies. First practiced by the wealthy planter class; and considered the white man's game. By the 1880's Gentlemen's Clubs flourished and blacks were not welcomed, and browns barely tolerated. Since then, Jamaican (West Indies) cricket, now the province of the locals, has grown in stature and produced such greats as George Headley, Frank Worrell, Gary Sobers, Courtney Walsh, Viv Richards and Brian Lara. The game has been responsible for breaking down the social prejudices that existed, and developing a national and regional source of pride for the Caribbean.

Dead Season: This was the term used to describe the period when there was no manufacturing of sugar, and when the slaves were used to check ratoons, repair equipment and Great Houses.

Deficiency Acts: This referred to the acts used to ensure that the ratio of blacks to whites was kept at a "safe" level.

Democratic Socialism: Policy of the Michael Manley led PNP Government of the 1970s, which caused great social upheaval of the society, and which failed with Michael Manley returning the PNP to Capitalism.

Devon House: Historic building which is regarded as one of the finest examples of 19th century architecture in Jamaica. The house was built in 1881 by George Stiebel. It has since been restored and the lovely grounds are a popular site for picnics and wedding photographs. Devon House is also now the home of restaurants, gift shops and other attractions.

Dinki Mini: This is a dance of African origin of the wake tradition and is usually performed after the death of a person and up until the ninth night of the death.

Distillery: The area of the factory where rum production took place. There were two forms of production, Pot Still which was used up to the 1900s and Continuous Stills. Pot Still rum is the heavier bodied rum (Jamaica) and Continuous Still, the lighter (Trinidad, British Guyana).

Dollar Diplomacy: Under this policy, the United States made significant financial investments to Caribbean countries in areas such as the railways, the sugar industry and the banana industry. The period from 1909 to 1913 is generally considered the era of Dollar Diplomacy.

Domestic Slaves: Slaves who worked in the Great House, i.e. nannies, butlers, cooks. There, slaves were usually regarded a higher status in the slave society and as such were (with few exceptions), never a part of any uprising.

Dreadlocks: The practice of Rastafarians not to cut or comb their hair as is forbidden in the scriptures.

Duho: The stool of the Arawak Cacique.

E

Economic Slave Control: Method of economics used to exercise total control over slaves, by providing them with everything they needed.

Emancipation: The freeing of the slaves in the British West Indies. The law that was passed by the British Parliament was called the Emancipation Act. It provided for freedom for the slaves from August 1, 1834, but with certain conditions attached under a transitional period of Apprenticeship. Full freedom for the slaves in Jamaica was not achieved until August 1, 1838, four years later.

Emancipation Day: This day was first celebrated to mark the freeing of the slaves on August 1, 1838. It was discontinued after Jamaica gained political independence in 1962, and was replaced by Independence Day, the first Monday in August. After a break of 35 years, Emancipation Day is again celebrated in Jamaica (since 1997) and Independence Day has been fixed as August 6th.

Encumbered Estates: Sugar Estates which became bankrupt after Emancipation.

Falmouth: The capital of the parish of Trelawny. The town is a historic site and is regarded as Jamaica's best example of Georgian era architecture and ambience.

Field Slaves: Slaves who worked in the cane fields. They were divided into three groups: the first was the youngest and strongest, the second were mothers and ill slaves, the third were old men, women and young children.

Federation: The attempt by the colonies to form the British West Indies into one trading block by forming the association of ten states between 1958–1962.

The Jamaican population voted against this proposal and because of Jamaica's strong economic base (at that time) the proposal failed. It prompted the late Eric Williams, PM of Trinidad, to observe "one from ten left zero". The ten states were – Jamaica, Trinidad, Barbados, Guyana, Antigua, St. Vincent, Dominica, Montserrat, St. Kitts and St. Lucia.

Free Black: Black persons who purchased their freedom from their masters.

Free Coloureds: Children of white and black parents in the slavery society.

Free Villages: Villages set up after 1838 by ex-slaves, numbering hundreds by 1850.

Fort Charles: A visitor attraction, is the oldest standing fortification in Jamaica dating from the English period.

G

Garvey, Marcus Mosiah (1887–1940):
Founded the United Negro Improvement Association (UNIA) in 1914 to advance the need to recognize Black Pride and consciousness, and give vision and meaning to our future. At one time he led the largest membership of any organization in the world.

Founded the first political party in Jamaica (PPP) in 1929. His attempt to give the Black man a voice in Jamaica was ridiculed, and consequent victimization and false charges led to his migration to the UK in 1935, where he died in 1940.

The Harlem Renaissance in the USA and the Pan African liberation movement in Africa, were greatly influenced by Garvey's philosophy, as is the Rastafarian movement. He was named the first National Hero of Jamaica in 1964 when his body was returned to the island from the UK where he had lived in exile.

Gordon, George William (1818–1865): National Hero of Jamaica, member of the legislative council in 1860. His vociferous defense of the conditions of the poor brought him in conflict with Governor Eyre, which led to his being accused as one of the leaders of the Morant Bay rebellion. He was found guilty and hanged in 1865.

Gordon House: Where Jamaica's House of Representatives meets. It is named after one of Jamaica's seven National Heroes, the Rt. Excellent George William Gordon.

Grant, Sir John Peter: First Governor of Jamaica (1866-1874); came after the Morant Bay Rebellion. Initiated reforms in social services (Rio Cobre Irrigation Project, Coronation Market, Jamaica Constabulary Force).

Great House: Home of the white estate owner – lavish structures of brick and limestone copying popular European architectural styles such as the Georgian Style.

Halse Hall: One of Jamaica's historic houses. The house is located in an area that had Arawak villages nearby.

Hammock: Sleeping device made by the Amerindians and slung between two poles. It was made out of cotton.

Hogsheads: Sugar barrels with holes in the bottom so as to allow the molasses to drain. It usually held 1000 lbs of sugar.

Holeing: Term used to describe the holes made in the newly tilled soil to plant cane stalks.

House of Assembly: Body responsible under the colonial rule for governance of the people. It almost always represented the narrow interests of the white population.

I

Imperialism: Policy of one country controlling another.

Indentured servants: Whites, Indians and Chinese who came to the West Indies on service contracts for five years during the 17th century.

Independence: The freeing of colonies to become masters of their own fate – Jamaica gained hers in 1962.

Indians: East Indians came to Jamaica between 1838–1917. It is recorded that this amounted to some 34,000.

Industrialization: The development of non-traditional natural resources, light industries and mechanization.

J

Jamaica: The longest English speaking country in the Caribbean. Jamaica is 150 miles long with almost half the island consisting of mountainous terrain reaching over 1000ft. high. Jamaica has over 120 rivers and there are over 3000 varieties of flowers that can be found on the island - 800 species of which are indigenous to Jamaica.

Jamaica Labour Party: One of Jamaica's two (2) major political parties. The JLP was formed on July 8th, 1943 by Sir Alexander Bustamante. On April 10, 1962, the JLP won the general election which was called to decide which party should lead Jamaica into independence.

Jobbing slaves: Term used to describe the artisans, blacksmiths, carpenters, masons and fishermen, who were hired out by their owners and had to share all if not most of their earnings with their owners. Some owners made their only earnings from these slaves.

Kingston: Became the second Capital of Jamaica in 1872 and remains so today. Kingston was founded in July 22, 1692 as a refuge for survivors of an earthquake that destroyed Port Royal. Today, Kingston is a bustling metropolis, one of the major business hubs of the Caribbean.

L

Letters of Marque: Permission letters from the French Government allowing privateers to attack Spanish ships, used also by the British and the Dutch to contain the Spanish economic wealth.

Limestone: Extensively used in construction of buildings and roads from the 19th century.

M

Manley: Norman (1893-1969) Considered one of the founding fathers of modern Jamaica. Founded the PNP in 1938 –

**THE RT. EXCELLENT
NORMAN WASHINGTON MANLEY, Q.C., LI.B.**

National Hero, and former Premier (1959-62) Chief Minister (1955-59).

Manley: Edna (1900-1987) Artist born in the UK, married Norman and bore two sons, Douglas and Michael.

Manley: Michael was Prime Minister in 1972-80, and again in 1989-92. He propounded the teachings of Democratic Socialism.

Marley, Bob: World-renowned reggae superstar and semi-religious icon. Bob Marley was the universal ambassador of Jamaica's renowned reggae music. His songs of resolution, rebellion and justice, finding audiences worldwide. Numerous books have been written about his life. The platinum-selling superstar died of cancer in 1981.

Manumission: Process by which slaves could purchase their freedom.

Maroons: Enslaved blacks who fought the British from their deep mountains, having gained their freedom from the Spanish

EDNA MANLEY

masters when Britain attacked in 1655. They were the first people to defeat the British in a war. A Treaty with the British gave the Maroons the lands on which they lived. The Treaty also gave the Maroons the responsibility of assisting the British in capturing runaway slaves.

THE LATE GREAT BOB MARLEY

MAROONS IN AMBUSH
(COURTESY OF THE NATIONAL LIBRARY OF JAMAICA)

Marson, Una: Journalist, poet and broad-
caster, leading exponent of femininity,
black civil rights and West Indian
Literature – worked with the BBC.

Mento: A very distinctive indigenous musical
form which represents the Jamaican folk
culture. Mento has many distinguishing
features, including the accent of the
fourth beat of the music. Instruments

used in mento include the guitar, banjo and rhumba box.

Mercantilism: Economic policy implemented by the European powers in the 16th and 17th century, which confined trade with the colonies to their respective mother country.

Mico: Established in 1836 to train teachers. It was created out of the Mico Charity, a trust created by Lady Jane Mico with £1,000 willed to her nephew in 1666, who failed to meet the preconditions. When the investment grew to £120,000 by 1834, the Trust was restructured and the funds used to build elementary schools.

Middle Passage: Second leg of the triangular slave trade. Slaves were chained and packed into the holds of the ship in tight body-to-body positions with no access to any form of human need. They were rarely taken on deck during the 4 – 6 week journey. The weak and the sick were thrown overboard. On arrival, the survivors were doused with sea water, rubbed with oil, given haircuts and pieces of cloth. For the women it was later referred to as the shame cloth.

Militia: Small armed forces of free men used to quell uprisings.

Mills: Used to extract cane juice from the cane stalks for sugar production. One of three types was generally used – water mills, windmills, or animal powered mills. The steam mill was later introduced.

Molasses: Product of sugar production process.

Morant Bay Rebellion: Led by Paul Bogle. What started out as a protest march on October 11th, 1865 to protect the harsh conditions in Jamaica and the low wages (Starting at Stony Gut to the courthouse in Morant Bay), turned into a rebellion when the courthouse was burnt, the Custos killed, and shops looted. Martial law was invoked and Bogle and George William Gordon were sentenced to death. A later investigation led to the recall of Governor Edward Eyre.

Mother Country: Name given to European country who had colonies in the West Indies.

Moyne Commission: Established to hear evidence of economic and social conditions in the West Indies. It recommended the financing for the colonies to improve health, social welfare and the promotion of Trade Unions.

Mulatto: Term used to describe children of a black and white parent, often white planters and black mistresses. The children were known as free coloureds. Other gradations of colour were quadroon and mastee.

Nanny: Made a National Hero in 1975. She was leader of the Maroons Wars. Nanny Town in Portland is named after this brave warrior.

Nationalism: Pride and commitment to one's country.

Non-conformist Missionaries: Christian denominations which parted from the Anglican Church (Baptists, Wesleyans, Quakers, Presbyterians, Methodists) who all played a major role in the abolition of slavery.

Obeah: Religious practice of the slaves from West Africa. It is the practice of casting spells on victims for good and evil.

Overseer: White person in charge of the daily operation of the Plantation and by extension, the slaves.

P

Panama Canal: Built by the USA (1904-1914) to link the Atlantic and the Pacific Trade Routes, started by the French in 1883. Returned to Panama in 1999. It was built by thousands of labourers with Jamaicans, Barbadians and St. Lucians playing a major role.

STREET IN PORT ROYAL
(COURTESY OF THE NATIONAL LIBRARY OF JAMAICA)

Peasantry: Ex-slave population who planted ground provisions (yam, etc.), owning land from one-eighth to five acres.

Peasantry Also known as free villagers.

Penn, Admiral: Captured Jamaica from the Spanish with General Venables.

Pepperpot: Soup originally made by the Arawaks. It is a mixture of meats and vegetables. The meat is boiled until it is tender, then the vegetables are added and is left to simmer for a minimum of 15 minutes.

People's National Party: One of Jamaica's two major political parties. The Party was formed in 1938 by Norman Manley. The PNP has been in power for an unprecedented four terms.

Pirates: Persons who would steal and plunder ships at sea and were usually citizens of European nations. Port Royal became the main city of host (wickedest city on Earth). Henry Morgan became Lt. Governor of Jamaica in 1671.

Plantation: Acreage devoted to sugar cane, usually vast acreage and by its way of life gave rise to the Plantocracy.

Plantocracy: The white slave owning members of the society.

Pot Still: Used to make rum in the distillery. This process ensured a high alcoholic strength.

Port Royal: Home to the Pirates of the Caribbean. It was destroyed by an earthquake on June 7th, 1692.

Puncheons: The name for oak barrels with charred insides, used to aid the process of aging rums.

Quadroon: Descendants of a white person and a mulatto, distinctions of the slave era.

R

Rastafarianism: A religion born in Jamaica in the 1930s at Pinnacle in St. Catherine with Leonard Howell as its founder. It accepts Haile Selassie of Ethiopia as the Messiah.

Reggae: A musical form developed in the 1960s and was a direct child of the Ska. It grew out of social experiences and had as some of its main exponents, Bob Marley, Jimmy Cliff, Toots Hibbert and Count Ossie.

Ratoons: The young sugar cane shoots that grew back after the ripened (matured) sugar cane was reaped.

Referendum: 1961 – held in Jamaica to decide if Jamaicans wished to remain in the West Indies Federation.

A RASTAFARIAN

Remittance: Money and goods sent back to the West Indies (Jamaica) by emigrants overseas; now the 2nd highest foreign exchange earner for Jamaica.

Reynolds, Mallica (1911-1989): Self taught artist, described as the father of 'intuitive' art; also known as the shepherd or leader of St. Michael's Apostolic Church – a Revivalist Church.

Rum: Alcoholic beverage made from cane juice and or molasses, using the fermentation process and distillation.

S

Sailing ships: Vessels of the 15th and 19th centuries which carried all the goods to the West Indies.

Scramble: Slaves were brought to a selling area and the ultimate rush to choose the healthiest and strongest was called a scramble.

Seaga, Edward: The Right Hon. Edward Phillip George Seaga served as Prime Minister of Jamaica 1980-89 and was the leader of The Jamaica Labour Party from 1974-2005. He has the distinction of being the longest serving elected Member of Parliament, having served for over 40 years. He is also Chancellor of University of Technology and Fellow of University of the West Indies.

Seasoning: Attachment of a new slave to an already broken one, and the process by which the new slave became acclimatized.

Selassie, Haile (1892-1975): Worshipped by the Rastafarians as the Messiah/Jah – crowned Emperor of Ethiopia in 1930 – Haile Selassie I Might of the Trinity, King of Kings and Lion of Judah – direct descendant of Solomon – Read 'Kebra Negast' – Miguel Brooks.

Sharpe, Sam (1801-1832): A National Hero of Jamaica and Baptist lay preacher who led the 1831 Christmas Rebellion. Known as Daddy Sharpe to many. (He led non-violent protests). Was put to death

SHIP IN PORT ROYAL HARBOUR
(COURTESY OF THE NATIONAL LIBRARY OF JAMAICA)

on the 23rd May, 1832 by hanging in the Montego Bay Square – Read 'Samuel Sharpe' – CS Reid).

Ska: Musical form developed in Jamaica in the 1950s which used the banjo as part of its rhythm. Proponents of the music were Millie Small, Byron Lee and Edward Seaga.

Slave: A human being who was the legal property of another human being. The majority were black Africans captured and brought from West Africa to the West Indies.

Slave driver: A slave who was put in charge of other slaves.

Slavers: Specifically designed ships used in transporting large numbers of slaves (used in the Middle Passage).

Sligoville: First free village in Jamaica, founded in 1835 by Reverend James Phillipo.

Squatting: Living on lands owned by the Government without expressed permission.

St. Jago de la Vega: The Spanish name for Spanish Town, the 1st Capital of Jamaica. Named by the Spanish, and founded in 1534; remained the capital until 1872.

Sugar: Made from the juice of the sugar cane. The juice was boiled into a sticky substance (molasses) and exported to Europe.

Sugar cane: Tall stalks or fronds, growing up to 20 feet in height, when reaped it was processed into sugar.

Sugar factory: Area used to manufacture sugar, rum and molasses.

T

Tackey: Leader of the slave rebellion in St. Mary. He was formerly an African chief in Ghana before his capture.

Tackey's Rebellion: Led by Tackey in 1760, led to the slaying of 60 whites and 300 slaves.

Taino: Amerindians who populated the Greater Antilles.

Tobacco: Smoked by the Amerindians. It was a native plant to the Americas.

Tourism: Early 20th century industry developed out of the Banana Industry when the cargo ships were fitted with accommodations (1890-1910).

Trash House: Building used to store the cane trash, which was then dried and used as fuel for the boiler house (also called bagasse).

Treadmill: Torture instrument used to punish slaves.

U

UNIA: United Negro Improvement Association formed in 1914 by Marcus Garvey. Its objective was to spearhead the effort to give the black population pride and vision.

Universal Adult Suffrage: Constitutional rights of all persons over the age of 21 to vote in elections – obtained by Jamaica in 1944.

United Fruit Company: Established by Capt. Lorenzo Baker in 1899 – established Railways – Steamers and Hotels (Titchfield, Portland).

Vacuum Pans: Covered boilers heated by steam that were used in the manufacture of sugar.

Venables, General: Defeated the Spanish in 1655 in Jamaica and with Admiral Penn played an important part in keeping the island of Jamaica for the British Crown.

Water mill: Used to extract cane juice; built when the water from rivers was used and sent to the plantation via aqueducts.

Wattle & Daub: The method used to construct buildings during slavery. Sticks (wattles) and daub (clay, dirt, leaves or straw) were placed in a frame-like structure which formed the walls.

Wilberforce, William: Vocal abolitionist who fought in opposition to slavery.

Z

Zemis: Statues of Arawak Gods; used in religious ceremonies.

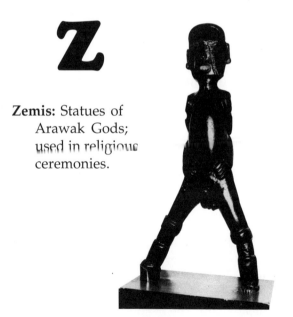

(COURTESY OF THE NATIONAL LIBRARY OF JAMAICA)